DOGS STAY

CHRIS SHEA

**Andrews McMeel**
PUBLISHING®

Dedicated to
the clowns,
the heroes, the
true companions
of our hearts.

Dogs Don't Die
DOGS STAY

Andrews McMeel Publishing
a division of Andrews McMeel Universal
1130 Walnut Street, Kansas City, Missouri 64106

www.andrewsmcmeel.com

19 20 21 22 23 SDB 10 9 8 7 6 5 4 3 2 1

ISBN: 978-1-5248-5335-8

Library of Congress Control Number: 2015933196

ATTENTION: SCHOOLS AND BUSINESSES
Andrews McMeel books are available at quantity discounts with
bulk purchase for educational, business, or sales promotional use.
For information, please e-mail the Andrews McMeel Publishing
Special Sales Department: specialsales@amuniversal.com.

STAY

for Ben

STAY

That's what dogs
do

because that's
what God designed
them
to
do.

(God said it first.)

" STAY "

"Good dog!"

He gave
them
all that they
need
in their
endless
pursuit

of
every
good thing

on earth.

Blue rubber
bones,

chew toys that
squeak,

and a soft,
   comfy bed
    for
      sleeping,

a sunny spot
for digging,

a shady spot
for resting,

and

" Yes! That one."

a person to
love
forever,

the one their
itinerary
Compels
them
to
Find.

We teach
our dogs
to
speak
and
sit,

or bring back
    the
    ball
    we
        throw.

But better far
than what we teach
them
is everything

A - Z
Things
to
TEACH
OWNERS

they teach
us:

unconditional love,
unconditional devotion,

Uu

unconditional

(adj.)

not limited
in any way

(like dogs'
love)

and loyalty
that
never
ends.

We give them food to eat,
    water to drink,
  a treat to chew,
and a place to
      Sleep
    at night.

They give us
Something greater...

a reason
to get up
in the morning.

Then one sad
day,

it appears that they have left,

and we have to
say
farewell

to our four-legged
forever
friend.

And if we
forget their
sweet
itinerary,

We are left to
wonder
where they are.

Dogs don't die . . .

they stay

because loyalty,
   companionship,
   and
faithfulness
   last forever,

just
as
God
designed
them.

" Stay. "

We see heaven
in the
eyes
of our
dogs,

and they find it
at our
feet

in a love affair
that never
ends.

Then comes the
thing that dogs
will do

when they
  think
  we're
  ready :

they find us
another dog to love

because they know
we've reached the
place

where the house
is far too clean,
way
too
quiet,

and unbearably
dog-less.

And one day,
out of the blue
when your heart
is on the
mend,

your old dog
will fetch
for you

another dog
to
love...

☆ forever...

another
dog
who'll
STAY.